glaciology

CRAB ORCHARD SERIES IN POETRY
Open Competition Award

glaciology

POEMS BY Jeffrey Skinner

Crab Orchard Review &
Southern Illinois University Press
Carbondale

16 15 14 13   4 3 2 1

The Crab Orchard Series in Poetry is a joint publishing
venture of Southern Illinois University Press and
Crab Orchard Review. This series has been made
possible by the generous support of the Office of the
President of Southern Illinois University and the
Office of the Vice Chancellor for Academic Affairs and
Provost at Southern Illinois University Carbondale.

**Editor of the Crab Orchard Series
   in Poetry: Jon Tribble**
**Judge for the 2012 Open Competition
   Award: Cynthia Huntington**

Library of Congress Cataloging-in-Publication Data
Skinner, Jeffrey.
[Poems. Selections]
Glaciology : poems / by Jeffrey Skinner.
pages cm. — (Crab Orchard series in poetry)
"Open competition award."
ISBN 978-0-8093-3273-1 (pbk. : alk. paper)
ISBN 0-8093-3273-6 (pbk. : alk. paper)
ISBN 978-0-8093-3274-8 (ebook)
ISBN 0-8093-3274-4 (ebook)
I. Title.
PS3569.K498A6 2013
811'.54—dc23   2013011886

Printed on recycled paper. ♻

The paper used in this publication meets the minimum
requirements of American National Standard for
Information Sciences—Permanence of Paper for
Printed Library Materials, ANSI Z39.48-1992. ∞

For Luci & Josephine

Contents

Acknowledgments

abz: "de Kooning"

The American Poetry Review: "Queue," "The Wedding at Ram Island," "Frame," "Signs & Portents," "All Things Move toward Disorder Except the Newly Created," "Theodicy," "Exit Row," "Stutter," "Give Me Poland," "Prayer for My Daughters"

Columbia Magazine: "Icon," "The Deal"

Connotation Press: An Online Artifact: "Kafka, Women"

Diagram: "Glaciology"

Fence: "Shattered Bio"

The Kenyon Review: "Ode to a Photographer"

The New Yorker: "Reunion"

Ploughshares: "The Fly"

Plume: "Throw It All Away"

Poetry: "Votive"

Quick Fiction: "The Mission"

Sentence: "The Children's Table"

Slate: "I've Been Working on the Railroad," "Self-Made"

Sycamore Review: "Jonquillity"

Valparaiso Poetry Review: "Event Horizon"

Whiskey Island: "You Need a Subject for the Sun to Rise"

Some of these poems also appeared in *Swerve*, a chapbook from Pudding House Press, and *The Execution of Little Maude*, an e-chapbook from Scantily Clad Press.

I thank the National Endowment for the Arts, the MacDowell Colony, the University of Louisville, the Kentucky Arts Council, and Tirbracken Farm for support that made the writing of many of these poems possible. Thanks also to Dick Allen, Mark Jarman, Leslie McGrath, Robert Pinsky, and, as ever, Sarah, for help with this book.

To be a child is to see things and not
know them; then you know them.

—Frank Bidart

Shattered Bio

Once I walked a thin rail through a glacier.
The lime-blue water could've killed me.
I considered it.

For a long time children were my music.
Squeak of pine trees in a forest.

Blue drug night, kneeling.

Let's fasten our openings together,
Love. A man can eat only so much dolphin soup.

Pinwheel, the baby's hand.
Corridor of scars lit by kerosene flowers.
Picnic with corn, snap peas, relatives in saran wrap.

I have been hired by divine gangsters—
Reason my work is invisible.

Queue

The line for immortality's long, longer than the DMV's, and you hear
The same jokes about eternity. New people join every day, of
Course, and it's amazing to see the young hop on in such numbers—
We always for unfathomable reasons believed the line would end with us.

Up ahead the kindly and the brutal alike keep disappearing.
And all along the line's horizon you see men and women step away,
Out of boredom or a fit of sense. The sun, a child born bronze in the grass.
Night rolling in its fields of stars and planets. We sing, we wait.

I've Been Working on the Railroad

I've always had trouble with the boss, even when I was self-employed.
Why do I have to sit there for eight hours when I can finish the day's
work in fifty-seven minutes? And there was a flaw on the face
of the office clock, a flyspeck or mole between five and six
where the eye went naturally, as if to the corner of an otherwise
impeccable woman's lips. I kissed that flaw in my mind, over and over,
because I had nothing else to do. The idea of work is fine, but
must we put every idea into practice? The trees, which I sometimes
catch waving to me, seem content in every weather, as if they
were continuously employed actors, and when the script calls for caress
the willow bends and draws its leaves delicately across the grass;
if violence, the oak twists and snaps, the palm leans back its heavy head
in the storm, frond-hair whipping madly. On the other hand trees
are never permitted to leave the office. I have been working so long
I forget sometimes what job I'm doing, and instead of teaching
grab my students by the belt and collar and stack them floor to ceiling,
thinking I am back at my cement factory job. What's amazing
is how little they complain, and my evaluations come out nearly identical
to those times I actually teach something. Perhaps in the end all work
is equally forgotten, and the transmission of knowledge a long train crossing
Kansas at 3 AM, a glowing tube full of dreaming passengers.

Ode to a Photographer

Pictures of developments half-built, white PVC pipes
Jutting like bones from denuded ground, workers
Feeding branches to a chipper, halogen-lit mounds
Of sand at night, men smoking in front of the justice building,
Landfill mountains of plastic and torn fabric and animal
Decay, Walmart parking lot, barges bearing slag
Down a godless river, new building facade still covered
In Tyvek plastic panels, work crew shearing crumbled
Concrete balustrades from the one-lane bridge . . .
He would check the items off his list of ugliness
After each shoot, having only one rule: he could not
Choose frames for beauty, only truth. He swore he knew
The difference. It was more than enough work for a lifetime.

Frame

There is always something left out of the poem
if the subject is darkly broken then joy
if joy then Ecclesiastes in his green visor
leering   from the margins   even if you try to leave

no margins and push the font to the edge
and over   letters lose arms   legs and heads
then it is those arms   legs   heads left out   for example
an old man in a train station who has forgotten

which train what city all he has done
and the woman selling tickets feels sorry and brings
coffee and a blueberry scone so he smiles
but says nothing as if expecting

even this   the poem has opened now
to the old man and the speck of compassion
which pulls the frame down from the continental view
one room   green tile walls   yellow bulb

the poem is a hand tool a hammer
of perfect heft good for house and garden
useless for large scale movements of earth   or troops
cannot change a river a planet a fatwa a bone

you must kill the poem in its crib for those
you must get on the train as a young man and not return

The Wedding at Ram Island

For Leslie & Bill

Amtrak, church bell, fog horn. Promises as buttons
come undone. The tick of aluminum masts
in the harbor, the beautiful bride standing in the sea.
Why, when there is no suspense, do we love ceremony?
After seeing what happens to us, to the earthly,
visible part. Trying to pick up water
between two fingers. Still, we marry. Three dogs

and two cats, a troupe of itinerant acrobats—they've
lost their leader. After bursting into a room
with nail-ticking fanfare, their tricks seem random,
sweetly odd—here a leap onto a table,
there a licked knee. Meat on the kitchen island, pounded
and spiced. The hypertext of teenage speech
ricocheting off tile. Adults hunker amid the clatter,

talking books, real estate. From the front porch
I see the blue glitter of the sound through massed branches.
Though I was not at the wedding, I can make out
the bride, standing in the sea. The owner of an island
never dies. You see the sheep grazing there, believe again
the story of the world. Our rituals try on eternity.
The pit bull smiles like a black lantern.

The Children's Table

I speak of a table made of children. Except for the top, which is made of glass. The children learn to present as many flat surfaces as possible to receive and securely balance the glass. They are permitted to talk amongst themselves in that *sotto voce* whisper only children can hear. Anything louder invites correction. If one must relieve him or herself the others shift to support the increased weight.

A children's table. A table made of children.

For them the hardest part is keeping still. It is better since the execution of little Maude, who had a particular problem with movement, and was incorrigible. Now the adults sit and talk for hours, directing the table to be placed as the pleasures of weather dictate, from the veranda when autumnal and sere, to the observatory at night when it snows, whitening the black bubble.

What do we talk about? Anything we please, though we have banished the topics of insurance and illness. Such talk invites aging, black and white dreams, and the music of waiting on hold. No, at the children's table our talk is fresh, supple as a universe without fixed laws.

What was it like in the old days, before the pressing nearness of our own deaths caused us to abandon sacrifice? Hard to remember. There are videos but, so grainy, so boring.

Oh love, it is you and me now.

Exit Row

You love the shame of sex,
how it must be broken
each time to pull the
ecstasy lever.
Money's fine, kids
have found work. You
understand what
you are meant to do.
Lucky fuck,
you even score a seat
in the exit row. But can
you still muscle
that door into space?
If not, get up,
let someone else take
your place. Every one of
the dead wants what you have.

Kafka, Women

We went to buy furniture in Berlin. When I am kind,
Felice approaches. I fumble for the door. I suggest the axe
of marriage. This illness, feeling its way inside me.
Heavy furniture that looked as if, once in position, it
could never be moved. Grete, come to
the hotel, we will make plans. There's never this kind
of trouble at the brothel. Without my head
I would not be lonely. But it is so crowded, knocking
at my skull. Felice, I am ruin. The sideboard in particular—
a perfect tombstone, or a memorial to the life of a Prague official.
Do you love me, a little? I can obey everything,
except what is demanded. If during our visit to the furniture store
a funeral bell had begun tolling in the distance
it would not have been inappropriate. How can I write
amid the noise and smell of human bodies?
The dress you wear in my mind is disappearing.
Still I cannot see you with clarity. What have you done
with your gift of sex? Disease has taken up residence,
soon there will be no room for Franz. I yield not a particle
of my demand for a fantastic life. Marry me, Felice.
Save me. Leave me alone.

Coffee

Everything has its mouth to manifestation . . .
                              —Jakob Böhme

Then what does matter
mean if nothing
matters? You answer,
blood moves & we
keep waking, my pet, my
back-handed hope—
the point's moot.
Back of my hand: blind
side that never blisters
from the rake, nor
tracks the creamy slope
of pleasure. The diner blinds
divide & welcome
a buttered morning light
to flare on railback
chair & pyramided
silver tops of sugar jars—
almost makes you dream
it all starts up again.
The truth is it does &
it doesn't. I put my mouth
to manifestation's
clay lip, my lips to sun
sliding across the wine-
dark, oily surface of
today's brew—*Galata Kulesi*
Cuvee, then into me.

de Kooning

When I came to the Springs I made the color of sand.
I had three pots for the gray waters, many for the beach grass
and the green-gray grasses of the marsh. When a man turns
sixty he begins again, Goethe said. I did. I had Susan
in the low-ceilinged rental and Lisa near, with Joan. Elaine,
who could make of any place a Siberia, far—far enough. The doors
arrived wrong, but I kept them anyway, painting
the sexual gash at eye-level: Woman, Sag Harbor. I liked the canti-
levered glass walls of my dream ship, the twin boilers'
stainless huff below decks, the removable plate
in the hull to offload murals. My people had the sailor's
water love, and I was no different, though I couldn't swim.
I thought once of learning, for Lisa. All is metaphor, yah, sure.
But what I like best is the wet surface of paint, wood curling
from a plane's tucked blade. A woman, undressing.
They say I'm slipping. Maybe I am . . . the way I arrived
in this country, without a ticket—hiding in the heat and metal
soot with the workers. Slow. Still feeding the enormous engines.

Terrors of the Night

I'll never shake this feeling of being
watched, nor the opposite—
abandoned. Awake, hearing
the drift of adult voices
up the stairs, mixed with jazz,
George Shearing, heart-
clasp chords of the vibraphone
like melting crayons, gin,
lime, tonic—that mix I knew
I would become. I was seven,
turning the strangeness of self
apart from others over
in my mind—*How can this* I *be* Jeffrey,
how can this Jeffrey *be?*
God was there, but so enormous
His body thinned until
He could not be seen. In my attic
room, all light disallowed,
dinosaurs hunched heavy-footed
on the shelf beside my bed,
waiting for me to close my eyes.
Then they would make their move.
They would devour me.

The Mission

Europe was in trouble again and I went over. I found her in a bar, lipstick charmingly askew, snags in her black stockings. I got a coke and joined her in the booth. *Call me Jean*, she said, and stuck out her hand. It was limp, thrilling. Listen, Jean, I said. I know we've had our differences, but I really. She put her hand on my thigh. And maybe I'm out of line here, but. She opened her legs and placed my hand. I just gotta tell you that, well, you're. She crushed her cigarette out on my other hand. Now, *that* was totally uncalled for. Then she passed out in my arms.

A taxi (or however you say it) took us to the address I found in her purse. The streets of course were made of water and it was a long trip. Her sleeping face in the moonlight, blue and white, like carved soap. . . . When we arrived a pack of Schnauzers yipped and swirled in front of the entrance to her building and, since I was carrying her, I may have stepped on a few. But so what. I was on a mission.

Inside, I tucked Jean in bed and looked around. The entire apartment seemed to be ticking. It was almost a comfort. Otherwise all was chaos: from bidet to kitchen sink there were tipped bottles and food containers, ripped foils of condom packets, English spanking videos, brochures promising a new career, etc. It *was* moving to see the many photographs of my family, at every stage of our lives, hanging on the walls. But these images were shocking, too: bourgeois realist, sentimental. Not at all what I would have predicted.

Nothing more could be done. I went to the bedroom to check on Jean one last time. She was asleep, her body splayed out on the bed, legs spread far enough to plainly advertise that she wore no underwear. I stood looking a long time, until the church bell rang, and I noticed a thick, braided darkness pouring in the open window. I lay down beside Jean and pulled her close. Shut my eyes. Her hair was like coal turning into diamonds—that long, that beautiful.

Self-Made

Before puberty I knew the *I*: Mowgli, Maris,
Boy shadowing Tarzan; Ethnographer of dirt kingdoms,
Scientist of worm and dandelion blow;
Impresario of The Ant & Beetle Circus, witness to twisting deaths
of caterpillar and moth (placed gently in the web
by hand). After puberty I no longer knew who came
and went within this *I,* but knew a woman
was somehow implicated; somehow a woman carried,
beneath her clothes, a major clue.
Everything I had I gave to seeing through that fabric.
I never believed in the social me—loathe to speak,
to intrude—though he did what he could.
On clear nights frost entered my definition, as did
the language I learned at work with men.
When my father died, his self exploded
invisibly. But I felt particles streak through my body.
I am accumulation, lust, barrels of Seagram's,
memory, a few grains only of selflessness. My children
were made, not begotten. They carry my letter
of recommendation in and beneath the skin—proteins, enzymes,
electrolytes. I have offered it all up for renovation
many times with a smirk and crossed fingers, once in earnest.
Every day I am forgotten, a new man.

You Need a Subject for the Sun to Rise

You need a subject for the sun to rise
You need a horse to make a shadow
You need bullets, money
You need an ocean to bride the wound

You need the god that needs you
You need black jam for heaven
You need a fist from the embalmer
You need red jam for earth

You need a new planet
You need thumbs to dredge the lake
You need monkey, happy evil, bone breaker
You need another few centuries

You need a hole punched in your need
You need discipline
You need shavings from the moon
You need a subject for the sun to rise

Signs & Portents

Where can we go these days to smoke
And listen to Nina Simone as people pass,
Examining the varied rhythm of gaits
And the hunger each implies?

There should be a body of water
Nearby, an ocean, lake, river—the taint
Of salt or fish mixed with diesel;
Chairs and tables of brushed steel

Or polished chrome; the coffee black,
Serious. This is shading European, I know.
But I want America to listen to
Walt, finally—to get lazy and lay back

On the jaded French divan.
Where in America can we go to kill
The people who need killing,
Instead of endlessly complaining?

Where can we buy connecting cable
To plug artists into the middle class
Without exploding? We'd also like sex
That admits its own pleasure—

Where is the bed or chair selling nothing,
Ready for our heat, weight, moisture?
O where in America can we lie
In the grass, arms crossed, and just look up

At clouds, without seeing signs and portents?
I mean before we die, and they make us.

Theodicy

A fresh grief bouncing in from satellite;
Sarah on the phone by the back windows,
The back of our house nearly all
Glass. She tries to be calm
For the husband of the friend dying
But he is breaking. The same
Raw words rise and assemble
Every day—in waves crossing thin air
On the way down to rooms private
Or public, hands gripping table edges
With sudden force, lights
Flickering inside—why not say it?—
Souls. Then a bird slams into the window
In full flight, a feathered punch,
Falls to the deck outside, three feet
From Sarah, who leaps up
And paints a shriek across the room.
It's a woodpecker, a downy,
Black and white, surely dead
From blunt illusion. "Get him away!"
Sarah yells, her hand cupped to the phone,
"Put him in the grass!" When I go
Look closely the bird is alive,
His wings bowed slightly and curved
Around him like a robe. His beak,
Surgical, thin, black, opens and closes.

One eye drifts back and forth in its
Socket dumbly, like the bubble
In a level. I wonder if I should
Move him at all—I don't want to make
His ending worse. Surely it is sin,
Whatever sin is, to add to suffering by hand.
But it's also hubris to believe
We are only *agents* of suffering—
Glass where there should be air. Locked
In mind, we suffer more by mind—
Knowledge of endings before
Endings. God is mute in the middle
Of this argument, and in the
Beginning, and at the end. Aleda
Shirley is the woman's name; poet, wife,
Daughter, friend. Husband Mike's
Been all love for her for years, then years
Of illness, then love for days
Left now, weeks at most. Sarah, off
The phone, gives me the hapless rest. She'll
Call other friends we share, then
We'll all wait, holding what we know.
The universe weighs less. Though it means
Nothing—strictly speaking, it's a story—
Here's the ending: the bird vanishes.

Jonquillity

The word *jonquil* flutters to the page
It is no longer alive but doesn't know that
At first I cried, because my father's face
In the coffin was not his face

Later I rode my jonquil to the river
Sculls went by like arrows with thin legs
I joined the old men looking at the river
They said the wounds in my side

Were breathing holes, keep them open
We watched a girl with hair the length
Of her body step into a jonquil
Hair spread across the wake behind her

I folded my jonquil into a psalm
The old men laughed and spit sunflower seeds
A black dog leapt and paddled after
Whatever his master threw into the river

I piloted my jonquil to the funeral home
We went in to choose the music and the silk
My father got the director to laugh
Immediately a jonquil sprang to his lapel

Reunion

Why do you keep returning,
alive, able to walk and gesture as you could not at the end,
your movements sketchy, more holographic
than warm? Thanksgiving dinner with all the relatives
and I alone with the suspicion I cannot speak:
You should be elsewhere.
Heavy drinking, as always. The newest baby
passed around like a contagious glow. Same teasing of the strong,
same muffled terror of the uncertain.
All the while you, at the head of the table like a signal
carried by a frayed wire—there, gone, there—raising a glass
to toast, the rim never touching your lips.

The End of Striving

Once or twice in a fit of calm
I thought I understood—
enormous music from the blue
between clouds. It's harder
now to hear & hearing
includes less angelic, more
human cries. I would address
God in poems to show
how continuous the circuit
remains, but prayer meant to be
overheard must stink
of strut, the last thing God
needs. On the way to the gym
I broke my reading glasses.
I did not twist hard, only
cleaned with a T-shirt hem
as usual, *& bam*, they snapped.
Since reading on the bike's
all that makes sweat bearable
I may as well head home,
the clouds bunched up now &
scowling. Besides—I said to no one—
I'm calmer when I don't
work out. Weaker, & calmer.

The Barber

How fine the back of that boyish head
Traveling backward in the mirror, infinitely.
The smaller and smaller heads are fathers
The man never knew, receding
Back to the first—so tiny it's not there.
But the barber is there, who started it all.
He doesn't say much. He didn't always cut hair.

This is our island. It's a good island.
Until the grown-ups come to fetch us we'll have fun.
                        —William Golding, *Lord of the Flies*

Glaciology

1

John called and we met by the turtle fountain, dropped
into woods and ran rapidly the leaf-deckled path. Since we had been
together in the womb it was not always necessary to speak
to know the other's thoughts. We ran for an hour and broke from shade
at the railroad tracks, crossed and entered Blue Dog. Hungry,
John ordered the thick, Bible-black bread, open-faced, egg on top,
over easy. I had the same. All right John I said where have you been

all these years. Well he said as a glaciologist I have to be
where the glaciers are. One project can last years and run right into
the next, if the glacier cooperates. Last Fall out at Siple Dome
we measured the temperature of the ice stream by inserting
thermistor strings into the boreholes and letting them freeze in.
Then waited. We were after the deuterium content. But
equilibration takes time. Waiting is everything, don't you think?

No I said, not everything, and ordered more coffee.
Well said John you should perhaps spend some time in the cryosphere
yourself so you know what the fuck you're talking about. John
I said you're the glaciologist, chill. I thought then that we
may fight, that I would have to kill John, or he would kill me.
Then the waitress came by and I knew by the way he talked to her
he had heard my thoughts, and we paid and left.

2

I know nations must pretend to be people
I know people can't be squeezed into happy alliance

All earthly ice is hexagonal, the six-sided snowflake

I know every time I solve the earth
I leave my mind

Ice rivers flow slower at the bottom and edges
Faster and heavier in the center

Comes unbelief, after unbelief, decadence

Near the melting point, the surface contains many dangling broken bonds
Which promote the existence of a liquid-like layer

I know this, knowing little

And the low friction of many materials on ice: useful for Jurgen's sled
And skiing, and skating

Sintering of snow

I leave my mind

3

John I'm sorry your father died, and the other one died,
the one you called father.

Men are just fire.

Someone left the light of intelligence on
all night. It's not bright enough

to threaten sleep.

John I'm sorry the earth melts away.

4

The next day we met again and played pool in the afternoon.
The high ceilings and air conditioning and white walls
made the place breathe around the green felt the balls like atoms
clicked and we drank beer with submerged shots of Bushmills, we smoked
cheroots with white plastic holders. Mario came in wanting
to challenge anyone to trick-shot Horse, and John said sure, though

I sent hard thoughts to him which he somehow ignored.
John lost but everything was good humored and we kept drinking.
John I asked him later when we were sitting alone
do you imagine a definable point to it all, do you see anything
outside the books we have read and discussed, digested and excreted?
Why are you being such a woman, John said

and we laughed and left that place for the Quonset Hut,
which at the time was still serving ice cream. After pistachio cones
John looked out over the city conveniently spread before us.
You know I lost everything in that game of Horse.
What do you mean everything. He said,
Everything. Does that include Cindy I asked. Yes, Cindy.

5

Ice stream C is flowing East to West.
The surface velocity near our boreholes was measured
along two profiles using repeat GPS positioning.

In stage 3 hypothermia, major organs
fail. Clinical death occurs. Because of decreased
cellular activity, brain death takes longer.

6

Then he came over to help me build a bridge or stairway
over or down the drop-off leading to the creek
and the ridge back up. The slope was sheer, and filled in
with junk cement and rock, meant as a stay against erosion.
But how to sink supports deep enough, and angled

in such jumble. I said John come inside, let's think about this.
We took drinks to the upper room and laid the plans
on the floor beneath the skylight. What if we
cut all the bamboo growing on your North side, John said
and latticed it through the debris, building up from what was

given us. Then what I asked. Then we can use the iron
from the giant statue of Lenin I bought in Prague
to fashion stairs. My daughter Laura appeared suddenly
and Honey I said, we're busy right now. She was younger than her photo-
graph, and I think a little in love. John smiled, and she vanished.

7

I said John, how can we be almost through with this life?

8

John said, Ice
has a unique property, called regelation:
melting of ice under pressure, coupled with adjacent refreezing

of melt-water at lower pressure.

This is the mechanism
by which a loop of wire can be pulled slowly through an ice block
without cutting the block in two.

9

At work I found a message
from Cindy saying I saw you with John
and thought of us all
in that other time,
sincerely. I thought *sincerely*
cold, though we had not spoken
in years. As I worked
through the day
I realized how many came to me
not in the realm of school
or words but beyond,
some region where everyone
founders, and I thought
where is *my* place
of help why do they not come
to help me and then,
ashamed: that I was grown
and the boy returned,
the boy who could never speak up
and so never got enough,
the dead boy.

10

Zone of ablation: where glacial loss
is greater than gain.

I consider language
mistreated these days, asked to explain itself
to justify at the same time it bears
meaning, to own up

to creation at the moment of use
only, and only *that* meaning

anyone pours in—

his alone,
another to the receiver.

And so on.

Equality of isolation, the fully mirrored present,
zone of wastage.

Whereas: the ability of math to model reality
outside interpretation.

Among the moraine
often a sticky form of clay—
Till—
called *gumbo*

may form spherical shapes
may roll around in the glacial stream
picking up rocks

then known as
Armored till ball—

the unaccounted
delight
language may take

in itself.

11

John said I am shipping out of Manhattan, a Swedish
research freighter called the *Bergschrund*. We're going deep
this time below blue ice, I may not return.
John was dropping books over the edge of the pier

into water shrugging its green shoulders at the jostle of tugs.
Not much for recycling are you I said. Everything
recycles if you're patient John said, letting
Marcuse's *Negations* open its pages and attempt to fly

before he let go. It did not. At some time in the past
I thought, I must have made a mistake, and now
I am living the wrong life. Weren't we born near this
water, I said aloud. But by then I was back, feeding the dogs.

12

John you are from the *sciences*, I am from the *humanities*.

But you are more *humane*—what we

Call a paradox.

The spine of Long Island is Wisconsin moraine.

Then why are we tempted to kill

Each other?

These waters, he said.

And weren't you born first. *Depends on what day*

You ask mom.

Her drift of mind. *Yes.*

It turns out, not everything is possible in America.

In Manhattan, maybe.

Is it some kind of father thing?

The suspicion our scheduled deaths will be worse.

13

Our airplane broke through a 2 m snow bridge and fell into a crevasse.
The recovery of the damaged plane took 6 weeks. One engine and two
propellers needed replacement. The crevasse
under the plane had been filled in before work started.
The LC-130 was finally winched out of its precarious position.
The BIG X on the image of Ice Stream D marks the place of the accident.

14

We were talking about women on the balcony during break.
Or, we were talking about language on the quay—
its obstinacy, its plush folds, its undiscovered pockets,

its dead ends. Big sun. A pelican came near
and John grabbed it by the neck and held it under his chair.
It was struggling and biting with its long clacking beak

and John I said that thing is tremendously strong,
you cannot take it home, it's likely to kill us on the drive.
Books and women, we were always talking books and women.

15

Freezing to death's
slow drift—

stage 3,
childhood returns

giggles,
white shade, soft opening—

mother,
mother oblivion.

16

Lord bless John's soul
Lord bless the weak
Lord bless the devil's role
Lord bless the words I speak

Lord bless the gray Atlantic
Lord bless shark
Lord bless a blue fanatic
Lord bless light and dark

Lord bless a woman's body
Lord bless father's eyes
Lord bless Cindy
Lord bless mortal lies

17

In his palm a peanut-sized, blood-flecked pellet.
Held out to me. What is it John. Take. This is what they

extracted from my right temporal lobe. A bullet?
No, too cold-growing: a crystallization. They were unable

to identify the source. Are you all right. Okay;
my judgment's off. When I sleep, the scar is visible.

18

I leave my mind.

Our moods do not believe in each other.

—Emerson

The Deal

The younger man is trying to sell
some project to the older man.
The younger man's hands move
over & above the maquette,
chopping the air here & there
in discreet emphasis. His
eyebrows lift to serious angle
at crucial moments of the pitch.
The older man mostly listens
but when he does speak
the younger man tilts his head
& leans in, squinting to read
all the older man does not say.
I can't tell if the sale is made
or not—smiles & handshakes
follow, but would in either case.
Of course my father pops
back into life at just that moment,
walking in the restaurant door
with his oiled athletic grace,
smiling like he has a new joke to tell.
But he ignores my presence
& sits down in my chair, in me.
Too obvious, dad, I say. Besides—
like I've tried to tell you my entire life—
poetry & business don't mix.

The Fly

The fly knows when I give up waiting
for him to land
and go back to my book.
Then when I am in the middle of a stanza or line
he returns, and just before
I am again aware
of his air-brake touch, he has bitten me;
I am jerked from the poem and the poem's world,
on the verge of transformation.

Miserable life, a fly's.
What is the point of fracturing and repeating
the world into a thousand images—
those bulbous, hairy,
coppery eyes? Little suckers for feet, veined,
cellophane wings. . . . Flesh-fly, sly fly,
vector of malaria, dengue,
yellow fever: Come back. I am sweet,
I have killed no one.

Icon

Who brings these messages
disguised as trees or vehicles
but which are in fact
people I once may, or may not
have known? Laurence
in his Big-Apple cap, & Nancy,
her peasant skirt flaring
as she closes her eyes to dance;
Chris, eating a plum & sweeping
the back stoop in Rye;
Frank Dunn, Wonder Bread
white & chubby in a cloud of blue
smoke, before the coffin
closed on so much less of him.
Time doesn't mess with these
faces, scrimshawed
cameos. . . . And what will god
think of next, I think
when the steel side of a delivery
truck throws a panel of sun
in my face, then guns it
around the corner. *Jesus* . . . I'm
back in the street again, facing
a tiny man made of light
blinking at me, telling me *Go
ahead now, it's all right to cross.*

When We're Done Writing about the Self

The breastfeeding mother has a cape
she puts wrong way over her head
so that baby can feed invisibly
in the tiny dark. The other woman
with the mother is fair, like
the mother, like the babies—
twins!—the one not feeding
content in the other woman's arms.
Sisters, maybe, the women talk
as they pass babies across
the table. Each bundle gets a turn
beneath the cape, emerging
whole, like a rabbit from nothing,
like a moviegoer from a matinee,
blinking away sudden light.
The women are in the early years,
baby rabbits at the beginning,
the man watching from a distant table
near the end. *Yes.* He considers
his long, silken ears, touches the alien
dryness of his face, & leaves.

Give Me Poland

Give me some ruckus in a minor key, some spacious yearning
Compressed into a cigar I can smoke on the beach. I like murmur
And lace coming toward me, otherwise black. Give me physics'
Best answer—is reality a scam, apart from consciousness?

Give me plunder and a woman, gold bars and a horse.
Give me a hat that announces how I'm feeling, so that when
I wear it people leave me the hell alone. But give me company
In labor. I won't care what happens when I'm dead—

I'll be so thin, so far off and transparent. Just leave one
Old song beyond existence. Give me names of flowers I can sew
In couplets, and walk among the rows in spring, tra la. Give me Poland,
I like Poland—how tough and smart, from so many beatings.

But promise, no more invasions. Give me a seat on the tram,
Young teeth, a smoky cafe, a blindfold. Give me Poland.

Corrections

A violet light addressed the snow
(*impressed, caressed, suggests*)—
this memory brought to you
by a boy in belled jeans
shifting foot to foot, impatient
to be off again. I believe
it (*he, I, you*) belongs to 1971,
when, after stubbing a jay
smoked in the furnace room
of mom & dad's, drifted
out & down into woods, to
the stream imperfectly frozen
(*stilled, cracked, shattered*),
ice plates like crockware stacked
in the mini-culverts, hard on
successive mini-falls.
Snow fluffed (*ruffed, bungled,*
plumped) the collar
of each bank, water like steel
champagne bubbled
the glassy vein. This someplace
else we're going, always,
is being's destination—
void at the hub, where God
pulses violet (*violent, voluble, silent*)
& the rest is snow.

Vintage Clock

It's making a wet grinding noise
as if someone had forced an extra gear
through its glass mouth & deep
into the works & now, useless,
unplugged, Futura numerals
& sage green metal frame
(childhood chic), tells lies all day
save twice—one second truths.
You stood two feet when
you & it were new, moving hands
& circled teeth hummed soft
high up the kitchen wall & grandma
walloped dough in mists of
flour, tarts appearing on steel
wire racks, mini-pies for cherubs.
It's tough to kill a thing
that's lugged so much time
into the present, but what can
you do? No one fixes anything
anymore, even if you could
find parts. Besides, that grinding—
presumptuous machine, mocking
our death rattle, rubbing it in—
go on, shoot it in the face.

Event Horizon

Saw the gravel edge,
The curve ahead—
One second expanded
Tire caught stone

Then all,
All slid from mind
And hand, then lovely
Resignation.

*

Loose container
Of fragments, bone
Parts afloat in gel
Pain closing teeth on

Nothing, eyes
Filled with ceiling tiles,
Gurney bumps. Brain
Burning the odds.

*

Lying still after
I.V. morphine, feeling
Blood velvetize the thousand
Tissue screams—

Blessing. Rising
Like a shaky scaffold
To crap in a chair by my bed—
Lord have mercy.

          *

Once, played Vladimir
In a production of *Waiting
For Godot.* It
Hurt, that part, it was

Too close to every-
Day, stripped
Of obligation. Please,
When will the doctor

          *

Come? I ask, or Sarah
Asks. But nurses
Don't know, phlebotomists,
Aides, housekeepers

Don't. The Docs'
Hands way too deep
In chests, heads, bowels, too far
From any pleading.

          *

My roommate's dying
Moans, grunts,
No no, no no no's
Steal more of my sleep

Than vital signs—
Blood sticks, B.P., dressing
Changes. Then *die,* I whisper
To the dun curtain.

Doug & Susan
Come, & Lucinda & Leslie,
& Rachel, & Alan, &
I get smaller

With each visit—
Farther away & harder
To hear, to see, until no one
Comes, I am not there.

*

Thought like a black
Seed in my head—I may
Not return. Grew,
Infected Sarah, who left

The sad room to scream
Inside the car. Sad
Room, may I go home,
May I leave before I leave?

*

Three tubes in my side
Coil to two
Blood boxes
By my side, chuffing

Bad fluid out
My chest. I feel each tube
Move as I move,
Dagger on bone.

*

Stitches snipped, needles
Removed—sent home,
Home to mend.
All shall be well, soon.

Dressing change daily,
Gauze packed
Like nettles in the wound
To keep it open.

*

Roshi said the people
In the plane crash
Are fifty percent responsible
For their own deaths,

The other fifty—
Nothing to do with them.
The rest of us shuttle between
One half & the other.

*

Mind keeps
The unutterable to
The margin—black stitching
Around a valentine—

True Love the cursive
Stitch wandering
The edge, while further in—
O Death, Be Mine.

*

Which is to say
My death so tiny
My death so intimate
My death so embarrassing

My death so chalky
My death so thin
My death so decorous—
Quiet in the hospital chair

*

Fever, & the tunnel
From infected
Fluid inside to bandaged
Skin—hot poison

Spurts each time
I turn or cough
Or laugh. Lucky the latter's
Rare, & rarer.

*

So much good
Was mine, an embarrassment,
A warehouse,
A loft of busy artists.

Is there a scale
That knows me, i.e., says
Hey, you've had enough,
Stand down?

*

God hauled in
Again for questioning—
Is this your work
By chance? No,

I'm well out of
That business. But you
Admit being at the scene?—
Among others, yes.

*

A week without
A shower
Because a walk across
The room ends in

Exhaustion, & water
Cannot touch
My wounds on either side.
Let me sleep, & stink.

*

Pre-op countdown:
Remove your
Rings & underwear.
Lie flat on the gurney.

Allergy to latex? Emergency
Contact, not your wife?
Living will, on file
With us? Comfortable?

*

Some nurses say *Sweetie*,
Others *Sir.* Some
Find the vein
Right off, others hunt

& poke. Some
Have healing faces, some
Soft hands. All
Arrive too late for pain.

*

Jesus, listen,
I don't know, I think
I have not been
This close to nothing,

I see now
How you live, the cold,
The invariance—I see your need,
Feel your likeness.

*

One can heal
And it is not sentimental,
Not a story for kids,
Not a myth—

But miraculous—
Orpheus returned
From the underworld, glad,
Head full of hell.

*

At the center
Sarah, then Laura & Bonnie,
Then Leslie, other
Friends, nurses, emails,

Cards, phone calls,
Flowers. Then
The grit I saved from childhood.
Sarah at the center.

*

To come back
After long illness—like switching
Gills to lungs,
All fours to walking

Upright—to be human
Again. I mean
The human of Mozart & Weil,
Not some airy phantom.

Stutter

a)
I feel there is something left to do
But can't get clear what it is;
I go around squinting into the next few feet ahead
As if instructions were just out of sight.

a)
I want to gather everyone I love
And arrange them by height in ascending order
So that I might step upward lightly
To make the drama of my death literal.

a)
I feel the trees are conscious
But the burden of thought falls to us.
The ways we see ourselves in the nonhuman
Express this gap, this loneliness.

a)
I want less and less, but what I want
I want with multiplied desire.
River, take what I lose to slag heaps,
What remains all the way to salt grasses.

a)
I want to write the last poem, the one
That removes the necessity to write another,
To retire without the sex of words,
Clear-headed, empty, free. No I don't.

Votive

If you wait long enough a sentence appears.
The how of this is helplessly entangled.
Something must be done about the filthy dark.
Every wick contains a number, the times it may burn.

Prayer for My Daughters

The sufferings of my daughters grow with years, trouble now adult-sized. The body shies, stands back, the mind stutters and fails. Come illness to them, uncertainty, sleeplessness, pain, lack of work making sense to them. When they call, the catch in their throat's my trigger—I want to jump through them into hurt and tear with my hands. Can't, sure can't. Then I think if we could huddle together again when they were small and I *did* place my body between them and things bulking in the dark we could find pure family, needing nothing. Was that it? Was it like that? Come happiness to them, come work and love enough to them. Come god I turned away from, come to them as you came to me, nevertheless. Set yourself in the place of sorrow, set them ablaze.

All Things Move toward Disorder except the Newly Created

My daughter is almost finished making a human being.
On that day, a singing will rise up through the surprised cry.
The likeness of god will have a fresh look at the universe.
None of her words are yet written, though she comes
With a language loom. She comes, the shock of consciousness
Waits. She comes, after light years of immateriality,
For the feel of skin on skin. No form is harder to enter
Than the human. The room is ready, the crib, the yellow curtains.
My daughter's heart is ready. The meadow where I pray,
The dogs. The river beyond, moving over and through itself.

Throw It All Away

My granddaughter who. The one alive in speech descends. A plate for Cali, a plate for Paul. The party of the first part, fallen asleep. How I wish, love, *you* know—we trade seed packets, we measure the silt turned dawn. Listen, when I stayed at the YMCA it was sadness married to a joke. It was frozen condiments, salt-packed meats, ethnography of the failed. Guess what: I'm thinking of a John Ashbery from one to a hundred. No grandchildren there. But a singular guitar, picked like a nose, a duck-like pluck. We learn other ways to be beautiful, don't we? And still the pure mouth, the child going away. A handprint works its silence down the chimney. Rain makes the lake a hammered steel. Granddaughter, pushing a blanket through the bars of political speech. Poetry a wind to lift new bodies from the earth. A happiness, a leaving.